For Rubin Pfeffer
and in memory of Hugh Weber
DP

To those who break all the rules, including their own
VT-K

First edition 2024

Library of Congress Catalog Card Number 2024932075
ISBN 978-1-5362-2032-2

25 26 27 28 29 30 TLF 10 9 8 7 6 5 4 3 2

Printed in Dongguan, Guangdong, China

This book was typeset in Adamina.
The illustrations were created using watercolor and digital tools.

Candlewick Press
99 Dover Street
Somerville, Massachusetts 02144

www.candlewick.com

EU Authorized Representative: HackettFlynn Ltd,
36 Cloch Choirneal, Balrothery, Co. Dublin, K32 C942, Ireland.
EU@walkerpublishinggroup.com

# LOVE IS HARD WORK

## THE ART AND HEART OF CORITA KENT

Dan Paley

illustrated by Victoria Tentler-Krylov

CANDLEWICK PRESS

**YOUNG FRANCES** loved making things. At home, she made paper dolls and their clothes. At school, she always volunteered to make the posters for events.

In art classes, she and the other students were taught to copy the Old Masters. Frances loved the chance to paint and create that art classes provided but longed for the freedom to make something of her own.

"Why don't you do something original?" her father prompted her.

Sister Noemi, her sixth-grade art teacher, also noticed Frances's innate talent and creative yearning and began giving her extra lessons after school.

Frances Elizabeth Kent grew up in a religious family. All of the children attended Catholic schools. Her older brother became a Catholic priest and her older sister a Catholic nun.

After her high school graduation, in 1936, and a summer spent at the famed Otis Art Institute, Frances herself entered the Roman Catholic order of the Sisters of the Immaculate Heart of Mary at Immaculate Heart College, a private college and community for women located in Los Angeles. For the next thirty-two years of her life, she lived and worked in this community.

The Immaculate Heart order
gave Frances the opportunity to
pursue the two things that were
most important to her: art and
religious life. She took inspiration
from religious art that depicted
stories from the Bible and from
medieval art illuminating Christian
history.
      She also loved words and began
to develop a style that combined
image and text, an interplay of
elements that would become her
signature style. The comfortable
familiarity of words, she believed,
helped draw people into a piece of art,
which might otherwise have seemed
impenetrable or inaccessible to
their untrained eyes.

When she entered the order, Frances changed her name,
a tradition that signified an entrance into a new kind of life.

Frances took the name Sister Mary Corita and began her career as an art teacher. The name Corita means

LITTLE

HEART

Sister Mary Corita taught her art students to open wide their eyes to see the world around them, to notice

# SHAPES
## AND
## COLORS
## AND
## WORDS

and to use what they saw as inspiration for making art.

She assigned innovative homework to free her students' minds from conventional thought and to liberate their creative spirits.

- Draw that chair a hundred times.
- Now forget the chair. Draw the empty space around it.
- Watch the shadows on the ceiling, how they move with the changing light.
- List fifty ways two peas from the same pod are different. And fifty ways they are alike!

When her students had mastered the art of learning to see, the hard work of turning what they saw into art began.

When what her students produced on the page didn't match what they had seen in their heads, Sister Mary Corita encouraged them to

KEEP WORKING.

If a student struggled to make perfect line drawings, Sister Mary Corita cheered her on:

**FORGET THE BRUSH! USE A TOOTHPICK OR A CHOPSTICK. A LONG STICK MIGHT LOOSEN YOUR GRIP!**

She taught her students not to get stuck attempting PERFECTION.

Sister Mary Corita and her students devised ten rules and posted them in the art department. The rules assured them something good would come from all their hard work.

**4** Consider everything an EXPERIMENT.

General duties of a student: pull everything out of your teacher; pull everything out of your fellow students. **2**

**1** Find a place you TRUST and then try trusting it for a while.

General duties of a teacher: pull everything out of your students. **3**

Be self disciplined. This means finding someone wise or smart and choosing to **follow** them. To be disciplined is to **follow** in a good way. To be self disciplined is to **follow** in a better way.

**6** Nothing is a mistake. There's no win and no fail. There's only make.

**7** The only rule is WORK. If you work it will lead to something. It's the people who do all of the work all the time who eventually catch on to things.

**8** Don't try to create and analyse at the same time. They're different processes.

**9** Be HAPPY whenever you can manage it. Enjoy yourself. It's lighter than you think.

**10** "We're breaking all of the rules. Even our own rules. And how do we do that? By leaving plenty of room for X quantities."
John Cage

HELPFUL HINTS:
- Always be around.
- Come or go to everything.
- Always go to classes.
- Read anything you can get your hands on.
- Look at movies carefully, often.
- Save everything—it might come in handy later.
- There should be new rules next week.

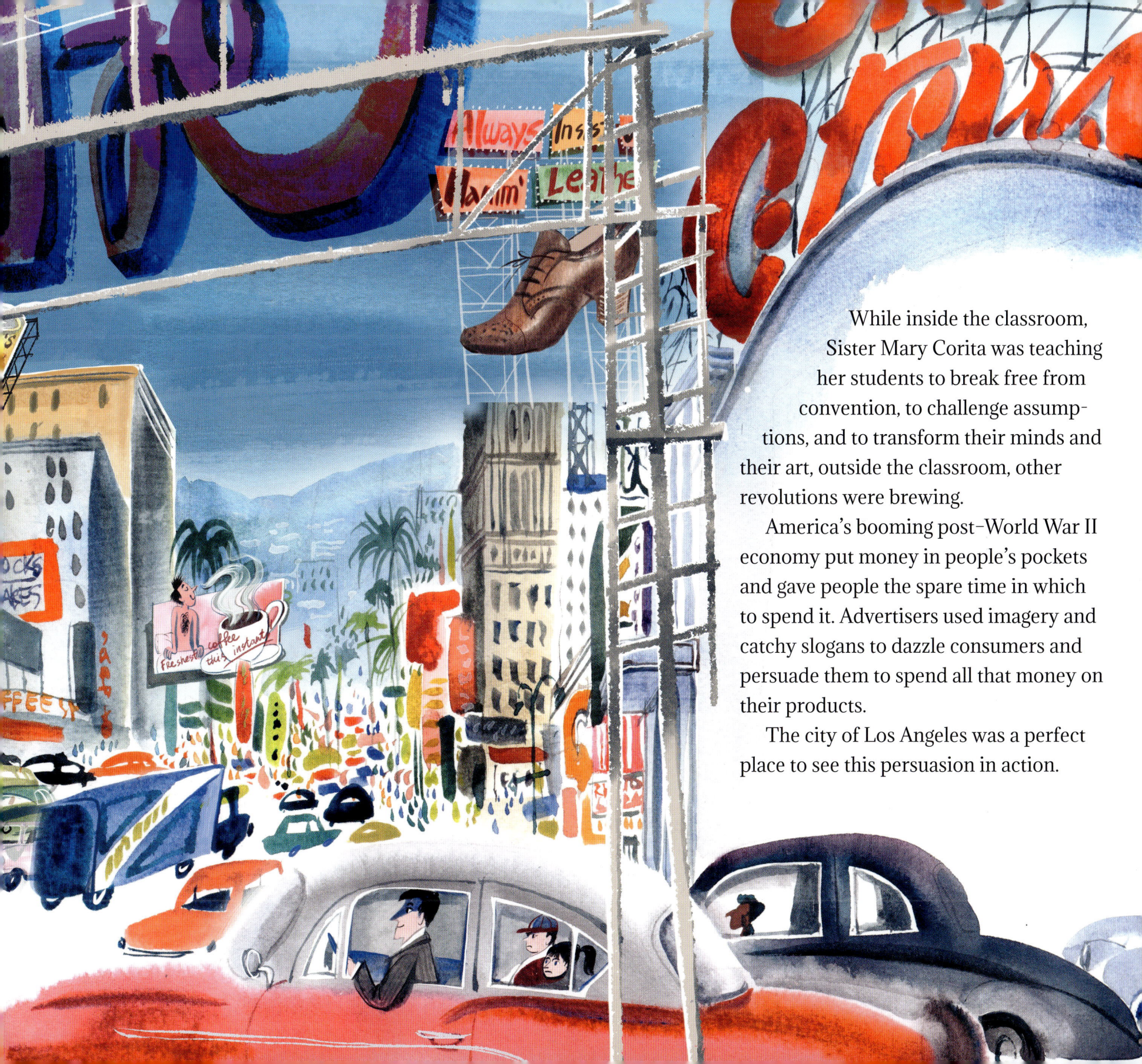

While inside the classroom, Sister Mary Corita was teaching her students to break free from convention, to challenge assumptions, and to transform their minds and their art, outside the classroom, other revolutions were brewing.

America's booming post–World War II economy put money in people's pockets and gave people the spare time in which to spend it. Advertisers used imagery and catchy slogans to dazzle consumers and persuade them to spend all that money on their products.

The city of Los Angeles was a perfect place to see this persuasion in action.

Sister Mary Corita had her students use homemade "finders" to isolate details in the sea of visual busyness. Like looking through a magnifying glass, such close examinations sparked fresh observations and led to new connections between disparate objects.

As a student of scripture—the sacred writings found in the Bible—Sister Mary Corita believed in the power of the written word. To her, words were divine. Words were the bread of life that sustained the human soul. She charged her students to take those words to and watch them COME ALIVE!

Sister Mary Corita was part of a generation of artists that redefined the role of art in society. At galleries and shows, she watched this evolution take shape. It was time for her to do something original. It was time for art plus action.

She would reclaim the words, colors, and persuasion used in advertising, not to sell products but to redirect people's attention to what she felt were more important ideas.

Sister Mary Corita's art alerted people to the fact that the postwar economic boom enjoyed by some was in shameful contrast to the poverty endured by others. She recognized that American ideals like

# LIFE, LIBERTY, AND THE PURSUIT OF HAPPINESS

were not equally or equitably experienced.

Using everyday objects and product packaging familiar to ordinary people, she not only challenged the limits of traditional fine art, but she also turned the trend of consumerism upside down.

While others marched or gave speeches, Sister Mary Corita protested with paint in the hopes of opening the eyes of others to all the injustices she saw: hunger, poverty, the suffering caused by the Vietnam War, inequality, racism, and civil rights abuses.

Through her art, Sister Mary Corita engaged with the overlapping artistic and social revolutions of the 1950s and '60s to spur change, change that she knew would take love and hard work. "To be fully alive," she once said, "is to work for the common good."

She used a technique called serigraphy, also known as silk-screening or screen printing, to layer text with graphics in order to shine a light on serious social issues.

POUR THE INK.

TRACE AND CUT A STENCIL.

SQUEEGEE ONE LAYER AND ANOTHER, AND ANOTHER, AND ANOTHER.

Song lyrics, scripture, poetry, and philosophy combined in Sister Mary Corita's heart and consciousness, filling her and spilling onto her canvas.

PLAY WITH THEIR

MEANING

TO MAKE

SOMETHING

NEW.

MAYBE DID SOMETHING

GO AWAY EVER SO QUIETLY WHEN

WE WEREN'T

LOOKING

E.E. CUMMINGS

TURN YOUR LETTERS ASKEW.

Big changes were also underway in the Catholic Church. In the early 1960s, the Second Vatican Council sought to make the church more relevant to more people. It switched from Latin to the vernacular—people's local languages—in church services, engaged with the challenges facing society, and worked to make the church more accessible to ordinary people.

For Sister Mary Corita, who whole-heartedly embraced such aspirations, it meant changing the way she dressed and creating art that brought the church's message into the modern era, sharing faith, hope, and love in a colorful new kind of scripture that the average person could understand and live by.

So when the church said to feed the hungry, Sister Mary Corita had the recipe. In one famous piece, she played with the iconic packaging design for Wonder bread, roughing up the brightly colored circles to make them look like the wafers received by Catholics during Communion, and pairing them with a hand-written quote by Mahatma Gandhi, an Indian revolutionary who inspired her.

In this way, she used her art to bring world hunger to people's attention.

But because Sister Mary Corita was a woman and an artist, and because she so enthusiastically took up the social causes of the day, she and the other sisters came to be considered a danger to traditions held by the conservative church leadership in Los Angeles.

Cardinal James McIntyre was a strict traditionalist and was among a few cardinals who attended the Second Vatican Council under protest.

In 1967, he barred the Immaculate Heart of Mary sisters from teaching in the city's Catholic schools unless they wore religious attire—called habits—and followed practices dictated to them, such as what time to go to bed and when to pray.

In 1968, while on Cape Cod, in Massachusetts, taking a break from work, Corita renounced her vows of service and retired from her thirty-two-year teaching career. The rigorous teaching and production schedule, combined with pressure to conform to tradition, had taken its toll on her, and in the end, she sought the more tranquil life of an

# artist.

She knew that making change, just like making art, was hard work, so for the next eighteen years, Corita continued making art that would wake people up. She believed art had the power to recognize people in need, to inspire action and change, and to be a source of hope and joy in a troubled world.

She opened the eyes of her students, her fans, and her fellow citizens to see what was possible, not just on the canvas but also in people and in the world.

Like the heroes she admired—Robert and John F. Kennedy, Pope John XXIII, and Martin Luther King Jr.—she did not fear the weather. She challenged the wind to blow more kindly over the world and its people.

She inspired artists and activists, teachers and designers to POWER UP for the work at hand.

Corita's bold message and art and her determined but gentle revolutionary spirit provide a unique window into history and a call to action in our own times.

Until the very end of her life, she shared her heart through art. It was a lifelong work motivated by love.

# AUTHOR'S NOTE

I was introduced to Corita's art in the home of a close friend, a graphic designer in Los Angeles, not far from the grounds of the Immaculate Heart Community and the Corita Art Center. As we ate lunch, I asked about a piece of art hanging on his wall. "That one is by Corita Kent," he told me. "Who is Corita Kent?" I replied. He went on to say that he had had the same question when introduced to her work years earlier. A friend of his had told him his work resembled Corita's, yet he had never heard of her.

That was the first thing I learned about Corita: that her work had a profound influence on the visual identity of the 1960s and has greatly influenced the fields of graphic design, advertising, and pop art, yet she remains largely unknown even in those fields. This is what inspired me to learn more about her and, ultimately, to write this book.

As I got to know Corita, I discovered a teacher whose method with students of all ages opened their eyes to what was possible, not just on the canvas but in their communities and in society as a whole; an artist who used color, perspective, and the written word to make the common uncommon; and an activist whose message of love and peace empowers us for the work ahead.

To learn more about Corita, visit the Corita Art Center online at www.corita.org.

# SELECTED SOURCES

Ault, Julie. *Come Alive! The Spirited Art of Sister Corita.* London: Four Corners, 2006.

"Corita Kent: American Printmaker and Pop Artist." The Art Story. https://www.theartstory.org/artist/kent-corita/.

Dackerman, Susan, ed. *Corita Kent and the Language of Pop.* Cambridge, MA: Harvard Art Museums, 2015.

Kent, Corita. "Corita Kent Oral History Transcript." Interview by Bernard Galm. Los Angeles Art Community: Group Portrait. Oral History Program, University of California, Los Angeles. 1977. https://archive.org/stream/coritakentoralhi00cori/coritakentoralhi00cori_djvu.txt.

——. *Footnotes and Headlines: A Play-Pray Book.* New York: Herder and Herder, 1967.

Kent, Corita, and Jan Steward. *Learning by Heart: Teachings to Free the Creative Spirit.* New York: Bantam, 1992.

Pacatte, Rose. *Corita Kent: Gentle Revolutionary of the Heart.* Collegeville, MN: Liturgical Press, 2017.

Rose, Aaron, dir. *Become a Microscope.* Nowness. 2009. Film, 23 min., 39 sec. https://www.nowness.com/series/directors-cuts/dc-aaron-rose.